Aulò! Aulò! Aulò!

ኣውሎ! ኣውሎ! ኣውሎ!

Ribka Sibhatu

Aulò! Aulò! Aulò!
ኣውሎ! ኣውሎ! ኣውሎ!

Translated by André Naffis-Sahely from the Italian
and from Italian translations of the Tigrinya and
Amharic made by the author

poetry
translation
centre

First published in 2020
by the Poetry Translation Centre Ltd
The Albany, Douglas Way, London, SE8 4AG

www.poetrytranslation.org

Poems © Ribka Sibhatu 2020
English Translations ©André Naffis-Sahely 2020
Introduction © André Naffis-Sahely 2020
Afterword © Sasha Dugdale 2020

Some of these poems first appeared in *Modern Poetry in Translation*, *World Literature Today*, The Brooklyn Rail's *In-Translation* and PEN America's *Glossolalia*.

ISBN: 978-1-9161141-3-5

A catalogue record for this book is available from the British Library

Typeset in Minion by Poetry Translation Centre Ltd

Series Editor: Edward Doegar
Cover Design: Kit Humphrey
Printed in the UK by T.J. International

This book has been selected to receive financial assistance from English PEN's PEN Translates programme, supported by Arts Council England. English PEN exists to promote literature and our understanding of it, to uphold writers' freedoms around the world, to campaign against the persecution and imprisonment of writers for stating their views, and to promote the friendly co-operation of writers and the free exchange of ideas.
www.englishpen.org

This publication has been supported by the European Union's Creative Europe culture programme which funds literary translations. The PTC is supported using public funding by Arts Council England

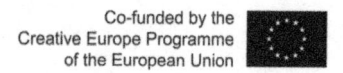

Contents

Introduction	7
Lampedusa	13
Now No One Sings Hosannas: An Open Letter	19
How African Spirits Were Born	21
The Exact Number of Stars	25
Virginity	33
My Abebà	35
African Grandmothers	37
Word	39
Mother Tongue	41
To the Sycamore	43
The Oasis	47
Prison Cells	49
Dear Rome	51
The Dubrovka Theatre	53

Eclipses	55
Afterword	57
Notes on the poems	62
About the contributors	64
About the series	66

Introduction

Ribka Sibhatu was born in Asmara in 1962, the year Emperor Haile Selassie's Ethiopia unilaterally annexed the former Italian colony of Eritrea, triggering a slow-burning liberation war that would last for the next three decades, with each of the then-superpowers, the US and the USSR, taking a side, turning the conflict into yet another Cold War proxy. In 1979, at the age of seventeen, Sibhatu was sentenced to ten months in prison for criticizing the government, on false charges trumped up by an Ethiopian politician whom Sibhatu had refused to marry. Upon her release, Sibhatu first took refuge at a relative's house, then adopted a false identity, finally fleeing to Addis Ababa in 1981, where she completed her education. In 1986, Sibhatu married a Frenchman, relocating to his native country, and she began a new life in Lyon, where her daughter Sara was born. Once that marriage ended, Sibhatu moved again, this time to Rome, where she published her first collection of poems, *Aulò! Canto poesia dall'Eritrea* (Sinnos, 1993), a volume of confessional lyrics written in both Tigrinya and Italian.

As readers will note in the following pages, works such as 'Virginity' and 'Prison Cells' starkly yet deftly relay the experiences and traumas Sibhatu suffered during her youth, offering us a highly intimate personal history, whether in the moving elegy 'My Abebà', written in tribute to a cellmate killed during Sibhatu's incarceration, or in the more light-hearted portrait of her daughter Sara at a young age in 'African Grandmothers'. Nevertheless, this selection also includes more overtly political poems, which see Sibhatu reflecting not only on her own deracination, or the plight of refugees, but even the fate of the Chechen separatists who stormed the Dubrovka Theatre in Moscow during the 2002 hostage crisis. Although

Sibhatu writes in Italian, Tigrinya and Amharic three of her five languages, the lost paradise of her native home always manages to sneak through, one way or the other. One may see this at work in 'Lampedusa', where the Tigrinya words of a desperate appeal to the Almighty tear through the fabric of the Italian original, a literal testament to Sibhatu's commitment to preserving Eritrea's culture heritage in exile.

Subject matter aside, what is clear to me about Sibhatu's work is that the author's uncompromising humanity is deeply embedded into each word, each poem of hers ultimately reconnecting us in both mind and heart to the wider human condition. I do not say this casually. On a visit to Lampedusa, roughly six months after 368 refugees drowned in the tragedy of 3 October 2013, Sibhatu painted the following picture of that southern island in an interview: 'I was struck to see how that tragedy had changed the lives of the Lampedusans. They were powerless before the enormity of what had happened, they had seen piers strewn with corpses, but I think that this tragedy brought us closer together. Both the parties involved experienced that moment in an overwhelming and violent manner, and despite the distance between them, they're both in mourning.'

Sibhatu's long-standing engagement as both a scholar and an activist no doubt helped shape her poetic work. Following a master's degree in literature and modern languages, Sibhatu then gained a PhD in communication studies from the Università degli Studi di Roma 'La Sapienza', later publishing her thesis, *Il cittadino che non c'è: L'immigrazione nei media Italiani (Invisible Citizens: Representations of Immigration in the Italian Media,* EDUP, 2004). Sibhatu worked as an intercultural mediator and consultant for Rome's city council in the early 2000s and has served as a committee member for various Italian ministries.

In addition to her work as a lyric poet and human-rights activist, Sibhatu has devoted a considerable amount of her creative energies to the assemblage and recording of Eritrea's folkloric canon, a body of oral literature which has been handed down through the ages in the form of 'aulòs' (literally 'Please give me permission! I have something to say publicly in rhyme!'), the Tigrinya term for chant-poems, or bardic songs, that are performed at public and private celebrations, as well as during religious rites. Her decade-long efforts in keeping these traditions alive – in the midst of her country's continuing unravelling and her work as one of the Eritrean diaspora's most indefatigable voices – finally led to the publication of *Il numero esatto delle stelle e altre fiabe eritree* (Sinnos, 2012), the title story of which is featured here in this selection. In these ancient aulòs, performers always begin their tales by invoking the word, 'Şinşïwai', which translates to, 'I have a story to tell', and to which the audience replies, 'Uāddëkoi şelimai', or, 'we're ready, we're listening'. During her youth, Sibhatu learned elements of this craft in Asmara, the capital, and Himbirti, her ancestral village in the high plateau, where these stories can be traced back for centuries. 'How African Spirits Were Born', also included in this selection, is popularly believed to be based on actual events and is thus performed without the usual introductory formula. Eritrean tradition holds that spirits can assume human forms and can be either malign or benign; for instance, the latter are thought to reside in pools of water, where people bathe in order to purify themselves and cure their illnesses. To this day, many claim to have seen spirits wandering their homes or villages, which explains why many are afraid to walk alone at night, lest they fall victim to spirits less kindly inclined.

I first began to translate Sibhatu's work in late 2010 and quickly found a warmly welcoming venue for this task when the PTC's founder, Sarah Maguire, commissioned me to lead a number of workshops on Sibhatu's wonderful poetry. As such, I am immensely pleased that the PTC decided to commission a small selection of my translations for their *World Poet Series*.

In her poem 'Mother Tongue' Sibhatu calls her five languages her stepdaughters and, over the past decade, I have received poems from her in Italian, Amharic, Tigrinya and French. The poems and fables included in this selection are presented first in their original language of composition, then in my English translation. The translations worked from Sibhatu's Italian versions of each work, or directly where the poem was composed in Italian. Although this is Ribka Sibhatu's first full appearance in English, I sincerely hope it is only the first of many.

André Naffis-Sahely

Poems

This book is dedicated to Abune Antonios, the Eritrean Patriarch, who has been in prison for fourteen years, and for all those who are in prison and died for our freedom.

It is also dedicated to my mother and father, whom I couldn't hug before they died, a price paid by so many Eritreans who take part in the struggle to defend human rights.

A Lampedusa

Il tre ottobre,
a Lampedusa è arrivato
un barcone con 518 persone.
   Sopravvissuti alla feroce dittatura
   e un viaggio pieno di insidia,
   nella notte fonda, dallo zatterone
   han visto le luci della terra promessa.
Credendo finita la loro sofferenza,
in coro, a gran voce, han lodato Maria.
Donne e uomini, adulti e bambini,
malati e sani, han cantato inni
aspettando i soccorsi delle due navi!

ስምኪ ጸዊዐ መዓስ ሓፊረ፤	Chiamando il Tuo nome non mi sono vergognato,
ማርያም ኢለ ኣበይ ወዲቀ፡	mi sono appellato a Maria e non sono caduto,
ስምኪ እዩእ'ሞ ስንቂ ኮይኑ፡	il tuo nome è stato il mio cibo di viaggio,
እንሆ ምስጋናይ ተቐበልኒ!	ed eccoti l'eco del mio riconoscimento, canto ad alta voce per ringraziarti!

All'improvviso, comincia
a riempirsi d'acqua il barcone;
per dare l'allarme, si accendono
e si spengono le luci rosse;
si accendono e si spengono le lampadine!
Purtroppo nell'isola, come prima, tutto tace.
Intanto l'acqua sale aumentando il terrore di affondare.
   Per dare un preoccupante segnale,
   si brucia una tela e divampano le fiamme;

Lampedusa

On October 3rd
a barge carrying 518 people
arrived in Lampedusa.
>   Having survived a brutal dictatorship
>   and a journey full of pitfalls
>   they stood atop their raft in the dead of night
>   and saw the lights of the promised land.

Believing their suffering had reached an end,
they raised a chorus to praise the Virgin Mary.
Waiting for those ships to rescue them,
men and women, children and grownups,
the sick and the healthy began to sing hymns!

ስምኪ ጸዊዐ መዓስ ሓፊረ፣	I wasn't ashamed when I called out Your name
ማርያም ኢለ ኣበይ ወዲቄ:	I called out to Mary and didn't fall
ስምኪ እፍአ'ሞ ስንቂ ኮይኑኒ:	Your name sustained me throughout my journey
እነሆ ምስጋናይ ተቐበልኒ!	and here is the grateful echo of the song I raise to thank Thee!

Suddenly the raft
started filling with water;
they started flashing
red lights to raise the alarm;
switching their lanterns on and off!
Alas, all was quiet on the island.
Meanwhile the water crept up, feeding panic the ship would sink.
>   They set a sail on fire
>   to signal their distress, and as the flames

alcune persone, spaventate dalle lingue;
scappando in massa capovolgono il barcone.
Tutti nel gelido mare!
Nella bufera, chi muore subito,
chi sfida il destino e la morte,
chi sa muoversi in acqua soccorre,
chi annega lasciando messaggi
da mandare nel proprio paese,
chi consegna ai vivi il suo nome,
e paese d'origine prima di morire!
    Tra i cadaveri che galleggiano,
    Yohanna! Yohanna! Yohanna!
    grida Mebrahtom disperato,
Yohanna non risponde;
ma in solitudine e un
estremo gesto d'amore,
tra i pesci, ha messo
al mondo il suo figliolo:
ma a Lampedusa nessuno ha sentito
i sette trilli eritrei di benvenuto!
        'ህአአአአአአአአአአአአአአ!'
Perché Yohanna è morta
dopo una lotta sovrumana!
il suo bimbo è morto senza
vedere la luce del giorno, è morto
prima di emettere il suo…primo respiro!
Un neonato è morto
soffocato dal mare salato!
Il bimbo è nato ed è morto
subito con il cordone attaccato!

began to spread, the most frightened
leapt overboard, tipping the boat over.
Then they were all adrift in the freezing sea!
In that storm, some died right away,
some beat the odds and cheated death,
some who could swim tried to help,
some drowned using their last breath
to send messages back to their native land,
some called out their names and countries of origin
before succumbing to their fate!
Among the floating corpses
Mebrahtom raised a desperate cry
Yohanna! Yohanna! Yohanna!
But Yohanna doesn't answer;
all alone, and in
an extreme act of love,
she brought her son into the world,
birthing him into the fish-filled sea:
yet nobody in Lampedusa
heard the seven ululations welcoming his birth!
'ሀδδδδδδδδδδδδδδδ!'
Because after a superhuman struggle
Yohanna died alongside her son,
who never saw the light of day
and perished without drawing his first breath!
A baby died
drowned in that salty sea!
The baby was born and died
with its umbilical chord still unsevered!

Una donna è mota mentre partoriva!
Sono morte 368 persone! Sono morti 357 eritrei!
 Il 3 ottobre 2013,
 nel cuore del Mediterraneo,
 a 800 metri dall'isola dei Conigli!
 si è consumata una tragedia del popolo
 eritreo; una delle tragedie del popolo eritreo.

A woman died while giving birth!
368 people died! 357 Eritreans died!
    On October 3rd
    3,000 feet from Rabbit Island,
    in the heart of the Mediterranean,
    a tragedy struck the Eritrean people.
    One of many they have endured.

'ኣበይ ኣበይ'ስ' ቀረ

የኢትዮጵያ ህዝብ በኣንድነት፡
'ፍትሕ! ፍትሕ!' ብሎ ተነስቶ ሳለ፡
ኣብይ፡ 'በይቅርታ እንታረቅ፡ በመፋቀር
እንደመር' የሚለው መፎክር ይዞ ብቅ ኣለ::
ህዝቡ ቃሉን ኣምኖ፡ 'ኣበይ! ኣበይ!' ማለት
ትቶ፡ 'ኣብይ! ኣብይ!' ማለት እንዲ ጀመረ፡
ኣብይ 'ኢሱ! ኢሱ' ብሎ ነገር ኣበላሸ::

'ኣበይ! ኣበይ!'ስ ቀረ 'ኣብይ ኣብይ' ን ተከቶ
በያረድ ዝማሬ የተቀነ የሰላምና ፍቅር ተስፋ ነግሶ፡
በዳዋት በገና ታጭቦ ወይ ሰሜን እንዲዘልቅ
ከሊቅ እስከ ደቂቅ ሲጠባበቅ፡ ኣብይ
'ኢሱ! ኢሱ!' እያለ ኖቤሉን ሲያካፍል፡
በመዲነቅ 'እንዴት መልኣከና ሰይጣን ተፋቀሩ?' ስንል፡
ህዝቡ መፈናቀል፡ ኣብያተ ክርስቲያናትን መስጊዶች
መቃጠል፡ ባንኮች መዘረፍ፡ ጀነራሎች መገደል ተጀመረ::
የሃይማኖት ኣባቶች ጤዛ ልሰው፡ ድንጋይ ተንተርሰው
የኣንድነት ታሪክ በደማቸው ጽፈው ባቀዲዋት ሃገር፡
የሞተው ሲገነዙ፡ ያዘነው ሲያጸናኑ፡ በገጀራ መቀረጥ
ብጥይት መገደል ጀመረ፡ ልጆቻቸው በፎቅ መዎርወር
ተገድለው መዘቅዘቅ፡ በእስር መማቀቅ ቀጠሉ::

'ኣበይ ኣበይ' ይባል ኣንዲነበረ፡ 'ኣብይ ኣብይ'
ማለትም እንዳይቀር፡ እንደ ኣጼ ቴዎድሮስና
ኣጼ ምንሊክ ስምህ ለታሪክ እንዲቀር፡ ሰው
ሁን ኣብይ፡ ሰው የሆን መሪ በተፈለገበት ሓገር::

18

Now No One Sings Hosannas:
An Open Letter

The Ethiopian people stirred and raised a loud cry:
'Justice! Justice!' and Abiy answered them:
'We must forgive and come together in the name
of love!' And so his motto won the people's trust
and instead of chanting 'Aboy! Aboy!' they began
to sing 'Abiy! Abiy!' but unfortunately, Abiy,
exulting 'Isu, Isu!', derailed the whole process.

When the people swapped 'Aboy, Aboy' for 'Abiy, Abiy',
hope soared for new and lasting peace, hymns
were sung, and all waited for the words of Saint Yared
to carry north in tune with King David's harp.
Then, when we saw Abiy publicly cheer 'Isu! Isu!'
we knew he'd betrayed his Nobel Prize, and reeled:
'how can angels and demons be friends?'
Next, his men started breaking up crowds, burning
the mosques and churches of our ancestors
who'd written the country's history in their blood,
who'd sated their thirst with dew, and used stones
as pillows. Now machetes slit the mourners' throats
who dared to wrap the dead, and the young
fall from windows or rot away in prisons.

Now no one sings hosannas to Aboy and perhaps the same
fate awaits Abiy; to find your rightful place in history you must
keep your word, and like King Menelik and Tewodros
be worthy of this great people you lead.

አፋጣጥራ ደቂ የሕድርትና

ሓደ ጊዜ ንኣፍሪቃ ብምልእታ ዝገዝኡ ለባም ንጉሥ ነበሩ፡፡ እዞም ንጉሥ ኣብ ዕብየት ምስ ቀረቡ ነቲ ዓቢ ወዶም ጸዊዖም፣

'ስምዓኒ ሚረን ወዳይ፡ ኣነ ናይ ስጋ ጉረ እየ፡ ሕጂ ግና ምስ ኣምላኺ ከተዓርቆ ከኸይድ እየ፡፡ እዛ ናተይ መዚ ግና ንስኺ ኣይትኽእላን ኢኻ፡ ንገመል እንተገፈፍኩሉ እዩ ዝሓይሸ፡፡'

'ኣይፋልካን፡ ኣነ ከለኹ ዓቢ ከመይ ጌርካ ነዉዑ ትሾሞ፡፡ ኣነ እየ ቦኺሪ፡ ንዓይ እዩ እቲ መንግሥትነት ዝግባእ!' በሉም፡፡

'ሓሲብካ ኣስተንቲንካ ዲኻ ትዛረብ ዘለኺ፡' ኢሎም ሓተትዎ፡

'እወ፡ ከምዚ ዝብለካ እንድሕር ዘይገበርካያ ፍትሒ ጎደለ ማለት እዩ፡' ይብሎም፡፡

'ድሓን በል፡ ካብ ኣበኺ፡ ፍርቂ ንስኺ ግዛአያ፡ ፍርቂ ድማ ሓውኺ ይግዛአያ፡'

ኢሎም ይምንኑ፡፡ ነብሶም ከፈቐዱ ካብቲ ሓያሎ ሃብቲ ዝሀሰሶ ናብራ፡ ቆጽልን ዝረከብዎ ፍረን እንዳበልዑ ንብዙሕ ዓመታት ምስ ጸንሑ፡ ሚረን ወዶም፣

'ኣነሲ ንዓይ ከሎ ዝገበኣንሲ ፍርቂ ሂቡኒ! ነዉዑ ቀቲለ ኣብ ኢደይ መንግሥትነተይ ዘይመልሰሉ ምኽንያት የለን!'

ኢሉ ቅድም ምስ እዛ ነብሱ ይዛረብ፡፡ ድሓር ሓዉ ጸዊዑ፣

'ሓወይ!'
'ዋሆይ!'
'ኣነ እንድያ ዓቢ፡'
'እወ!'

How African Spirits Were Born

Once upon a time, there was a strong, wise Emperor named Mersò, who ruled over the most powerful empire in Africa. When old age came knocking at his door, he summoned his first-born son, who was his designated heir, and told him:

'Miren, my son, hear me. I have nourished my body long enough and now wish to make my peace with God and tend to my soul. The art of governing and the sense of responsibility it has imparted me tells me you are not suited to the wielding of power and that it would be best if your younger brother Gemel ruled in your stead.'

'But this is absurd!' Miren exclaimed, 'I'm the first-born! How could you crown him in-stead of me?'

His father replied: 'Have you thought this through? And considered the consequences?'

'Yes!' his son answered, 'If you don't honour my wishes, there will be no justice in the Empire.'

'So be it,' his father concluded, 'I will divide the Empire between you.'

Thus, Emperor Mersò divided his realm between his sons, and retired from public life to lead a hermit's existence. Far removed from royal pomp, he spent many years devoted to prayer and dined solely on herbs, roots and wild berries: all in the quest to tend to his soul. However, Miren harboured great anger and resentment. But Miren still nursed a great anger and resentment and, finally overwhelmed by it, he decided to kill his brother and be recognized as the sole, undisputed ruler of the Empire. He paid Gemel a visit and told him:

'Brother!'

'Tell me,' Gemel replied.

'I am the eldest!'

'That you are...'

'ኣነ ከለኹ ዓቢ፡ መንግሥትነት ነዓይ ከሎ ዝግባእ፡ ኣቦይ ኣብ ክልተ መቓሉ ፍርቂ ንዓኻ ሂቡካ። ሕጂ ግና ነዚ ኩነታት ከቕድር ደሊያ ኣለኹ። ነዓኻ ቀለ እቲ መንግሥትነት ከጥቅልሉ እየ። ኣዘንጊዑ ወደቃ ወዲቋ ቀቲሉኒ ከይትብል ሕጂ ተዓጠቐ፤ እመጽእ ኣለኹ። ተዓጢቑካ ጽንሓኒ።'

ይብሎ ነቲ ንእሸቶ ሓዉ። እዘም ሰብኣይ ኣብ'ቲ ጫካ ከለዉ ኣምላኽ ይገልጸሎም። እዘም መንፈሳዊ ናብ ደቆም ይመዱ።

'ኣቴም ደቂ!'
'ዋሆ!'
'እንታይ ጎዲሉኩም ደኣ ኢኹም ጸላኢና ይጻላእ ትብኣሱ ዘሎኹም። ከተዓርቀኩም መጻእሁ።'
'ኣይተዓረቕን'የ! ዘየተዓረቐ ግብሪ እንዲኸ ጊርካ ኬድካ። እቲ መንግሥትነት ኣነ ከለኹ ከጥቅልሉ ዝገበ ኣኒ ምስ ወድኸ ፍርቂ ፍርቂ መቛልካኒ ኬድካ!' ኢሉዎም፡
'ኢልካ።'
'እወ!'
'ትኽእላ ደሞ።'
'ደሓን! ዘይክእላ እንታይ ኮይነ! ንሱ ኻባይ ዘብልጽ እንታይ ኣለዎ እዩ።'
'በል ሐረ፤ ብምልእታ ከትገዝእሲ ብሰውሩዶ ወይስ ብገልጺ ክትገዝእ። ኣብ'ታ ዝሓረኻያ እቶ!' ይብልዎ።
'ብስውር ከገዝእ እየ ዝደሊ!'

ይብሎም። በዚ መሰረት እቲ ዓቢ ምስ ህዝቡ ተሰወረ። እቲ ናብኡ ዝኣመነ'ውን ምስኡ ተሰወረ። ሕጂ ንሕና ንጻዓርናዮ፤ ንሕና ንደኽምናዮ ይበልዎ።

'And as such, I should have inherited all of the Empire. Instead, our father insisted on dividing it. Now it is time to rectify this: I want to kill you and seize all power for myself. But lest I be accused of subterfuge, prepare yourself for war. I'm coming for you.'

Even though he now lived in the forest, the heavenly messengers warned the old Emperor about what was about to happen in his lands. The old Emperor decided to visit his sons. Once he'd arrived, he told them:

'My sons.'

'Tell us', they said.

'What do you lack? Why are you fighting? I settled this matter before leaving you. Now I have returned to broker peace!'

'I have no wish to settle!' Miren exclaimed. 'Your decision meant there could never be peace! I should have been the sole ruler, but you forced me to share it with your son.'

'Is that your final decision?' his father asked.

'It is!'

'You wish to wield power alone?'

'I do!'

'Will you be able to handle it?'

'Of course, why wouldn't I? What does he have that I don't?'

'If that's the way you see it, then you must choose! Do you want to govern the visible world, or the invisible one?'

'If that's the way it has to be, then I choose the invisible world!'

And so it came to pass. From that day forward, the Emperor's eldest son and his followers became invisible: that's how African spirits were born, and ever since, they have fed on the food prepared by human beings.

ቁጽሪ ከዋኸብቲ

ጻውጻዋይ
ወደኮይ ጽልማይ

ብዘበን እኒ እኒ፡ ሐምባሻ ከሎ እምኒ ሓደ ርእሰ መላኺ ንጉሥ ነበረ፡ እዚ ንጉሥ ነቲ ሥልጣን ንበይኑ ደልዩዎ ዓበይቲ ዝኾኑ ኩሎም ሐርድዎም ኢሉ ኣዘዘ። ዓበይቲ ዝኾኑ ኩሎም ተሓሪዶም ከበቅዑ፥ ሓደ ጎራሕ ወዲ ነቡኡ ኣብ ትሕቲ መሬት ሓቢኡ ኣድሓነ። ነቶም ነቡኡ ከሓርዱ ዝመጹ ሽኣ፥

'ኣቦይ ቀደም እዩ ሞይቱ። ነባይ ኣደይ እያ የዕብያትኒ።'
ኢሎዎም። ሕራይ ኢሎም ከዱ። ቅንይ ኢሉ እቲ ንጉሥ ብዓለም ኣኪቡ እዚ ዝስዕብ ትዕዛዝ ይህብ።

'በሉ ቁጽሪ ከዋኸብቲ ሐጂ ትንግሩኒ።'
ኢሎዎም እቶም ዓዲ ተጨነቑ። እቲ ነቡኡ ኣብ ትሕቲ መሬት ዝሓብእ ወዲ፡ ናብ ኣቡኡ ከይዱ፥
'ኣቦ!'
'ዋሀይ!'
'እዚ ሓያል ንጉሥ ሎም መዓልቲ ዘይአዘዝ ትእዛዝ ሂቡና።'
'እንታይ ኢሉኩም'
'ቁጽሪ ከዋኸብቲ ኣምጽኡለይ ኢሉና።'
'ቁጽሪ ከዋኸብቲዱ ሓቲቱኩም እዚ ወደይ፡ ከትህብዎ ኢኹም ኣጃኹም!'
ኢሉ፡ ጣፍ ብዋንጨ ምልእ ኣቢሉ ሰፈሩ፡

The Exact Number of Stars

Şinşiwai! 'I have a story to tell!'
Uāddëkoi şęlimai! 'We're ready, we're listening!'

Once upon a time, when stones were made of ĥmbascāl bread, there lived a tyrant who couldn't suffer any threats to his power, and since this despot wanted to rid himself of any potential rivals, he issued an order decreeing that all the kingdom's elders were to have their throats slit, seeing as how they were the only ones who could pose a threat to him, employing the wisdom they had inherited from their ancestors. And so the kingdom's elders were slain. Only a single young man was able to save his father, building him an underground refuge where he could hide. When the murderers came looking for his father, the young man replied:

'My father died many years ago. I was raised by my mother.'
Without insisting further, the tyrant's men left.

After some time, the King called an assembly, at which he imposed a despotic demand on his subjects:

'I order you to tell me the exact number of stars right now!'

When the king's subjects heard this and understood how impossible it would be to oblige him, they grew very apprehensive. But the young man who'd saved his father immediately went to the latter's refuge and called him:

'Father!'
'Tell me, my son.'
'Today, the tyrant asked the impossible of us!' he said.
'What, my son?'
'We must tell him the exact number of stars immediately.'
'Did he really ask such a thing?! Take heart, you'll be able to give him the right answer!'

His father grabbed a wančia and filled it with a bunch of ṭaff, which he then spilled into a goat skin.

'እዚኤን ጣፍ አዚኤንን እቶም ከዋኸብትን ማዕረ ማዕረ እዩ ቀጽሮም፤ እዘን ጣፍ እንተደአ ሓሊፈን፡ ከዋከብቲ እንተ ጕዲሎም ንቅጻዕ::'

ኢሎም መለሹሉ:: ርእይ ኣቢሉ ሰብኣይ ሓፊሩ ትም በለ:: ህዝቢ እቲ ዓዲ ነዚ ዘድጋኖም ወዲ መሪቀም ንመራቂ ሃብዎ::

እቲ ንጉሥ ድማ: ቅንይ ኢሉ ሕዝቢ አኪቡ፤ 'ንስኻትኩም ትእዘዛዋ ኣሎኩም' በሎም:: 'እንታይ፤'

'ጸባ ብዕራይ ተምጽኡለይ!'

እቲ ህዝቢ ናይ'ቲ መንእሰይ ብልጋት እንምበር ናይ'ቦኡ ሕሳብ ምኜኡ ከይፈለጡ: ናብቲ ቅድሚ ሕጂ ዘድጋኖም ጎበዝ ብዙሕ ህያባት ሒዞም ተመልሱ:: ከም'ቲ ዝሓለፈ ከድሳኖም ብዙሕ ተማሕጸኑ:: እቲ ጎበዝ ብወገኑ ነቡሉ

ከምዚ ዝስዕብ ኢሉ ሓተቶ፤

'ኣታ ኣብ ሎሚ ከኣ እምበር ጸባ ብዕራይ ኣምጽኡለይ ኢሉና!'

'ዲሓን እዘም ደቀይ: ከተምጽኡሉ ኢኹም:: ሓደ ክብቶም ኣብዑርና ኣብ ሓጹር ሕጻርዎ: ንሾዉዓተ መዓልቲ ዝኸእል: እኽለ ማይ ክልእዎ፡ ኣብ ሻሙናይ መዓልቲ: ካብ ዝተፈላለያ ከብትታታ ብዙሕ ጸባ ሕልብ ኣቢልኩም ስጋብ ዝጸግብ ኣስትይዎ:: ደሓር ነቲ ብዕራይ ቀልጢፍኩም ከብኪብኩም ኣብ ንጉሥ ወሲድኩም ኣሽንዎ:: እቲ ዝደለዮ ጸባ ከሀቦ እዩ::'

ከምታ ዝበሉም ጌሮም::

'Here, my son,' he continued, 'these grains of ṭaff correspond to the exact number of stars. Deliver this goat skin to the King and tell him to count them. If there are more stars than grains, then we'll submit to any punishment he desires.'

The young man rushed to the assembled villagers and relayed his father's instructions, which were followed to the letter.

When the King saw what his subjects had brought him, he realized he'd been tricked. He was so embarrassed that it left him speechless.

The people were grateful to the young man for having saved the village. From that day on, his name was on everyone's lips and the young man was routinely blessed for all the good he'd done his people.

But before too long, the King summoned another assembly and said:

'I have a new request for you.'

'What is it?'

'You must bring me some bull's milk!'

The subjects were appalled by this new request and, as they didn't know who had really come up with the solution to their last problem, they went to find the young man. They brought him a number of gifts and begged him to solve this new enigma.

The young man went back to his father.

'Father, today the king made another impossible request. We must bring him some bull's milk!'

'Don't worry, my son,' the old man replied, 'Take one of our bulls, put him in an enclosure and keep him isolated. Deprive him of food and drink for seven days. On the eighth day, give him nothing to drink but milk. As soon as he's finished drinking, bring him to the King so that he'll pass the milk in front of his eyes. As you'll see, he'll pass nothing but milk!'

The village delegates executed the old man's recommendation and told the King:

'በሉ እነሆልኩም እቲ ጸባ ዝሐለብ ብዕራይ ኣምጺእናልኩም!'

ኢሎም ኣብቲ ጥቓኡ ጠጠው ምስ ኣበሉሉ፤ እቲ ብዕራይ ጀዲድ ኣቢሉ እንተሸየፈ፤ ጸባ!:: እቲ ንጉሥ ብዙሕ ተገሪሙ እንከሎ ኣጋይሹ ኣብሊዑ ኣስቲዮ ኣፋነዎም::

'እዋእ እንታይ ጽኣ ክእዝዞም እየ ኢሉ?' ክሓስብ ጀመረ:: ሓሲቡ ክስተትትን ምስ ቀነየ መሊሹ ኣቤባ ንኽግበር ይእውጅ::

'በሉ! እዛ ገዛይ፤ ሎሚ መዓልቲ፤ ከየነቓነቅኩም ኣብ ዝጠጠሓ ኣግዒዝኩማ ከምትጸንሑኒ::'

'ሕራይ! ዝዛዘዝምና ኩሉ ክንገብር ኢና::'

ኢሎም ናብ መገዱ እንዳሸዱ፤ ብልቡ ከምዚ ዚስዕብ ይብል፤

'ሕጂ ኸ እንታይ ምሂዞም ከንጉሑኒ እዮም!'

እንዳበለ ይኽይድ:: ከምታ ውዕሎም ድማ ፋዱስ ኣብ ገዛ ይርከብ:: ምስ መጾ እታ ገዛ ኣብታ ዝገደፋ ትጸንሖ::

'እዚ ገዛይ ከየነቓነቕኩም ኣግዒዝዋ ኢላ ከብቀዕ ንምንታይ ከየልዓልኩሞ ጸሒሑም!'

'ጎይታይ ከነልዕሎ ኢና:: ቅድም ቅድም ኣብታ ትቖመጠላ ቦታ ኣይነገርኩምናን፤ ድሕሪኡ ድማ ከተሸኩሙና ደሊና::'

'ነዓ እስከ ንስኻ!'

ይብሎ:: ነቲ ዝመለሰ::

'እቲ መጀመርያ መዓልቲ ንስኻ ከም ከዋኽብቲ ማእለውያ ዘይብሉ ጣፍ ሒዝካ መጻእካ፤ ደሓር ጸባ ዝሸይን ብዕራይ ኣምጺእካ፤ ሕጂ ኸኣ እነሆልካ ነቲ ብርቱዕ ሓቶ መሊሽካ:: ኣቦኻ ብሕይወቱ ከሀሉ ኣለዋ! ሓቂ ተዛረብ ወይ ድማ በዝ ሴፍ ክጎምዲካ ኢያ!'

'በሉ ከይትቐትሉኒ ቃል ኪዳን እተውለየ እሞ ምሥጢሩ ክነግርኩም::'

28

'Here you are, your Majesty, we've brought you bull's milk, just like you commanded.'

As soon as he'd been presented before the King, the bull started peeing milk. The King was astonished and regaled the village delegates with a sumptuous feast. All the while, he thought about what he might ask them next.

'What could I possibly demand of them now?'

After long reflection, he called another assembly and said:

'Hear me, my people. I want you to relocate my palace to a better spot, but I don't want a single item to be disturbed! And I want the task completed by lunch time.'

'Your wish is our command!' the delegates replied in unison.

After he'd communicated this latest request, the king left and thought:

'I'd like to see how they find a solution to this one!'

As agreed, the King went to meet the delegates at the appointed hour and, as he'd expected, found that his palace was exactly where he'd left it. He asked the delegates:

'I asked you to move the entire palace, so why is it still in the same spot?'

'Your Majesty,' they replied, 'We did move the palace, but as we didn't know where to put it, we placed it back where it was! Besides, we'd like you to rest it on our shoulders!'

At that point, the King lost his patience and told the man who'd conveyed the answer:

'You, come forward.' Obeyed, he continued, 'You were the one who brought me all those grains the first time; then you brought me a bull who peed milk and now you answered the most difficult question of all. There's only one explanation for this: your father is still alive! Either you tell me the truth, or I'll slice you in two with this sword.'

The young man replied:

'If you promise you won't kill me, I'll tell you everything you want to know.'

ቃል ኪዳን ምስ ኣተዉ፣
'እንበኣርከስ እዚ ኩሉ ምሥጢር ኣበይ ኢዩ ዝነገሪኒ፣'
'ዋይ ኣነ፣ ዓበይቲ ምቑታለይ ተጋግየ እንበኣር እየ!'
ኢሉ የንጸርጽር። ቀኒዑ ኸኣ፡ ንህዝቢ ፍረዱኒ ኢሉ ይሓትት። ዋላ ህዝቢ እንተ መሓሮ፡ ንሱ ሥልጣኑ ነቲ ኣቡኡ ዝሓብኤ ገዲፉ መኒኑ፣ ይበሃል።

ነዚኣ እንተረሳዕኩም ሞት ትረስዕኩም፡
ነዚኣ እንተዘከርኩም ሰንበት ሰንበት ገዓት
ጠስሚ የብልዕኩም።

The King promised he would do him no harm.

'What you said is true: my father helped us find the right answers to all your requests.'

'Poor me,' the King said despairingly, 'Our ancestors' wisdom truly is mighty. How wrong I was to have all the elders slaughtered!'

He subsequently spent a number of days reflecting on all that had happened and decided to submit himself to the villagers' judgement for all the evil he'd wrought.

Though the people forgave him, the King decided to give over his throne to the young man who'd saved his father, choosing a hermit's life to better tend his soul.

If you forget what you've heard,
death will forget you in your turn,
but if you keep on remembering,
may God grant you all the cornmeal you can eat.

ድንግልና

ኣብ ሃገርና ንሕልቲ መርዓት ድንግልናኣ ከም ዓይና ዘገድስ ክብሪ ኣለዎ። ምናልባት ካብ ዓይናኳ ይኸብር ይኸውን። ሓንቲ መርዓት ንጽሕና ድንግልናኣ ዝተደፍረት ኮይና እንተተረኺባት ኣብ ሣልስቲ መርዓት ወጮ ተኽዲና፡ ኣብ ኣድጊ ተወጢሓ፡ ብውርደት ንንዳቦኣ ኢያ ትምለስ። ብጊዜ ዕግርግር፡ ሕዝቢ ከተማ ኣብ ሃገረ ሰብ ተዓቚቡ ነበረ። ኣነባብር፡ ዝምርሓቚ ሃገረ ሰብ ብዙሕ ፃዕሪ ዚጥይቐ ነበረ፣ ንኣብነት፡ ዔላ ኣብ ክልተ ወይ ሠለስተ ኪሎሜትር ሰፈር ዚርከብ፣ እንተነበረ፡ ማይ ኣብ ሕቄኻ ተሰኪምካ እዩ ዚጉተት ዝነበረ።

ብ1981 ዓ.ም.ፈ. ኣብ ዓዲ ጓሙሽት ዝተባህለት ቁሽት፡ዚኣ ካብ ኣሥመራ ዕሥራ ኪሎሜትር ርሒቓ ትርከብ። ሓደ ኣጋምሽት ናብቲ ተዓቚቡሉ ዝነበርኩ ገዛ ኣርባዕተ ሸማግለታት ምስ ሓደ ርእሰዮ ዘይፈልጥ መልከዐኛ ጎብዝ መጹ። እቶም ሸማግለታት፡ ነቲ መንእሰይ ብድሮኡ መርዓቱ ሓሲማ ብምጽናሓ ዘጋጠሞ ሓዘግ ምስ ገለጹለይ ኣነ ክምርዓዎ ዝደሊ እንተኾይነ ሓተቱኒ። ኣነ "ንዘይፈልጦ ሰብ ኣይምርዖን" እንተበልኩሞ ኣዚኣቶም ምስ ኣበየ ድሮ ተሰማሚዕዎም እንተ ድኢ ኮይድሞ ወይ ከዝርፉኒ እዩም ወይ ድማ ኣበይ ኪረግመኒ እዩ። መረገም ወላዲ ኣብ ዓድና ብዙሳ እዩ ኢዮ ዝፍራህ፡ ሽዑ ሓንቲ ሓሳብ ተገልጸትለይ! "ኣነ ኸኣ ፈሲሳ ዘይተሓፈሰ ሓደጋ ረኺበ እንድየ" በልኩሞም፡ ናይ ኣቦይ ጓህነ ሀርቃንን ባዕልኻትኩም ከተግምቱዋ እግድፌኩም። ኣብቲ ማኣበረ ሰብነ ንሱውን በረኸት እግዚኣብሔር ከም ዝኃደሎ ሰብ ተቐጽሪ። ወይ መንእሰይ ድማ ኣፉ ከይከፈተ ካልእ ድንግልናኣ ዘይተደፈረት ጓል ከናዲ ተዓዘዘ!

Virginity

For a bride, her virginity is just as important as her eyes, if not more so. According to our country's traditions, if a bride isn't a virgin, she's taken back to her parents' house after her wedding and made to sit astride a donkey while wearing a wonciò. This is considered a disgrace for the whole family. During the war, people from the cities took refuge in the countryside and, in order to integrate, made many sacrifices. Many would shoulder twenty litres of water home even if the well was three or four kilometres away. By 1981, I was sheltering in Adi Hamuscté, about twenty kilometres from Asmara. One afternoon, a handsome youth and four old men showed up and they told me that the young man, whom I'd never seen before that day, wished to marry me because the previous day he'd suffered the misfortune of learning that his bride had been violated! If my father agreed with the prospective groom and I refused their proposal, I would have run the risk of being married off against my will, or worse, to be cursed by my father. Children greatly fear the might of their parents' curses! It was then that an idea occurred to me, which was to claim that I too had suffered an irreparable incident! I'll leave you to picture my father's reaction, whom was equally disgraced by my revelation in our community's eyes. The young man, for his part, went off wordlessly in search of his virgin!

እቡበይ

አበባ ጓል አሥመራ፥
ኣብ ሐዝሐዝ ሰፊራ፤

ኣየው... እቡብ ቅጭን፤
ዘረባኣ ኩሉ ብዕቅን፡
ከም ዓይንን ኩሕልን፤
ሐደ ሽማን መልከዓን።
ምስጢር ሞት ሓዚላ፡
ጋህሳ እናጬዓቱላ፡
ንዓለም ተአውዩላ፡
ሰደደት... ኣገልግል
ሕምባሻ ዘይበላ።

ለይቲ ምድሪ ካብ ጎድነይ፡
ብመጫሕ ተመንዘዐት እቡበይ።
....
ትመላለስ ኣብ ሐልመይ፡
ቀትሪ ቀትሪ ትገጽፊኒ በይነይ።

ካብ ኣበየት ካባይ ምፍላይ፡
ሒዛታ'ላ መልሲ ሕቶታተይ፤

'መዘከርታ ንወለደይ'
ትብል ኣገልግል እቡበይ
ኣምጹለይ፤
ናይ'ታ ከይ ዓምበበት ድዓረባ
እቡብ መተኣስርተይ።

My Abebà

On the hill of Haz-Haz
lived a girl from Asmara.
Alas... my beautiful Abebà,
so poised and slender;
Abebà, a flower that rhymes,
like Kohl around an eye!

So that the world may know:
while they dug her grave,
cloaked in mysterious death,
she wove an aghelghel
and sent it without hmbascià.

On an indelible night,
they handcuffed and kidnapped her!
....
Every day I feel her absence,
but I see her everywhere in the dark!

As she refuses to leave my side
bring me my Abebà's aghelghel:
perhaps it'll hold the answer,
the key to those handcuffs,
that now bite into me.

A single inscription on my Abebà's
aghelghel reads 'a souvenir for my parents',
a flower who withered before she bloomed,
my friend in prison.

Nonne Africane

Senza le ali
di un'aquila,
rassegnata ammira
la luna lontana,
coccola cani e gatti
senza chiederli più dove
stanno i nostri vicini.
Legge a casa e
a scuola, si chiede
come è fatta la terra.

Sara, non trovando
le scale per salire
alle stelle, non
vedendo Iddio
rispondere alle
sue domande; vuole
nome e cognome
delle nostre nonne
africane che Darwin
si dimenticò di
mettere nel suo elenco.

African Grandmothers

Lacking the wings
of an eagle,
resigned, she admires
the distant moon,
cuddling cats and dogs
no longer asking them
where our neighbours have gone.
She spends all her time
at home and school, reading
or asking how the earth was made.

Unable to find
the stairs to the stars,
and seeing that God
won't answer
her questions, Sara
wants me to give her
the names and
the surnames
of our African grandmothers
whom Darwin declined
to mention in his book.

Parola

Sacra Parola,
misteriosa essenza,
terra della straniera
che girovaga!

Tocca la figlia che
cammina tra
luci e ombra,
coraggio e paura.

Suona melodie
che danno forma
al mondo
a cui appartiene.

Parla parole ce
emanano profumo
e portano l'animo
nel tempo e nello spazio.

Word

Holy Word
inscrutable essence
land of the foreign
wandering woman!

Touch the daughter
who walks between
shadow and light,
courage and fear.

Play melodies
that shape
the world
to which she belongs.

Speak words that
emit a fragrance
and carry the soul
through time and space.

Madre lingua

Uno,
due, tre,
quattro, cinque…
Sono io e le mie lingue.

Le figlie adottive,
ora, son in maggioranza
e vogliono cacciare
la Signora di casa.

Come fa la tempesta
di sabbia al Sahara,
sballottandomi a destra
e sinistra, modellano me
e la mia Lingua Madre.

Sola e minacciata
la Madre Lingua,
cerca i Sicomori
e anziani prima che
svaniscano con i
loro tesori ancestrali.

Mother Tongue

One,
two, three,
four, five…
That's me and my languages.

The stepdaughters
now outnumber me
and want to chase
their Mistress out.

Just like the sand
storms of the Sahara,
they toss me to
and fro, shaping me
and my Mother Tongue.

Lonely and threatened,
my Mother Tongue
searches for lost elders
and Sycamores before
they vanish, along with
their ancestral treasures.

Al Sicomoro

Passati amari anni,
d'esilio e umiliazioni,
baciai prostrata Himbirti,
la terra dei miei avi
che mi portarono
per mano al Sicomoro.

Sentii discorsi rimati,
ai vivi e ai morti,
leggi e compromessi...

Poi svanirono dietro
il maestoso Sicomoro
recitando indicibili aulò,
recenti canti-pianti
e del lontano passato.

Era settembre,
tornando sola e triste,
dalle case e chiese
sentii profumi d'incenso
e canti di capodanno.

Da lontano
aspetto il richiamo
del Sicomoro.

To the Sycamore

After years of bitter exile
and humiliation, I knelt
to kiss Himbirti, the land
of my ancestors
who led me by the hand
all the way to the Sycamore.

There, I heard rhyming speeches
to the living and the dead in rhyme,
laws and compromises…

Then they vanished behind
the stately Sycamore
reciting unsayable aulòs,
howling-songs of the present
and distant past.

It was September and winding
my way, sad and lonely,
among houses and churches,
I smelt the incense
and heard the new year's songs.

Now, from afar,
I wait for the call
of the Sycamore tree.

Quando mi rispecchio
sul volto umano
di vivere mi vergogno.

When I see my reflection
in the face of humanity,
it shames me to be alive.

L'Oasi

Lungo il viaggio,
alla fontana del canto,
nonno Sicomoro mi cullò
coi profumati cori secolari
che fecero crescere i miei avi.

Protetta dal Sicomoro,
cantastorie del passato mistero,
nel cammino e nell'esilio
canto l'immensità
nell'oasi della *Scrittura*.

The Oasis

Along the journey
to the fountain of song,
grandfather Sycamore cradled me
with the honeyed, ancient hymns
that once nurtured my ancestors.

Sheltered by the Sycamore,
the bard of a mysterious past,
on the road, and in exile
I sing of infinity
in the oasis of Literature.

Le Celle

Le tetre celle dei
condannati, come
ieri, oggi, mi fanno
venire … i …brividi.

Come se fossi
ancora là, …sola,
che tremo e urlo
al sordo mondo,
la Sacralità della Vita!

Prison Cells

To this day, the bleak
cells of the condemned
send shivers down
my spine.

It's as if I
were still there, alone,
trembling and screaming
at a world gone deaf,
the Sanctity of Life!

Cara Roma

Cara Roma,
per i nuovi cittadini
una lupa non basta!

Ci sono: indiani,
russi, palestinesi
filippini; africani,
i figli di 'Lucy',
la lupa che generò
Romolo e Remo.

Cara Roma,
per i nuovi cittadini
una lupa non basta!

Dear Rome

Dear Rome,
one she-wolf isn't enough
for all your new citizens!

There are: Indians,
Russians, Palestinians,
Filipinos, Africans,
'Lucy's children',
the she-wolf that bore
Remus and Romulus.

Dear Rome,
one she-wolf isn't enough
for all your new citizens!

Teatro dubrovska

Sui divani rossi,
del teatro, donne
in nero, portano
bombe nel grembo.

Delicate mani,
incrociate sugli
schienali rossi,
non cullano
bambini ceceni.

Le donne del teatro
che portavano
bombe nel grembo
hanno partorito
un immane disastro.

Le donne in nero,
dal sonno privo
di sogno, in silenzio,
come se niente fosse,
sono svanite nel nulla
con i bimbi di Beslan.

The Dubrovka Theatre

Inside the theatre,
women dressed in black
sit on red velvet seats
with bombs in their laps.

Delicate hands
linked across
their backrests,
they nurse no
Chechen babies.

The women
who carried
bombs in their laps
have given birth
to a terrible disaster.

The women in black
who slept a dreamless
sleep, have vanished,
in silence, as if nothing
had happened, along with
the dead children of Beslan.

L'Eclisse

C'e' chi muore di fame,
o in pieno inverno dorme
per strada e chi vola da un
angolo della terra all'altra per
vedere l'eclisse a bocca aperta.

Eclipses

There are people who starve to death,
others who sleep rough in the winter,
and then there are those who fly from
one end of the earth to the other
to gape at eclipses.

Afterword

In 2016 Ribka Sibhatu's poem 'Lampedusa' appeared in a *Modern Poetry in Translation* issue I edited on refugee poetry. 'Lampedusa', in André Naffis-Sahely's translation, was the unforgettable opening poem of a selection of writings on flight and exile from all over the world. Ribka's poem takes the form of a lament for the dead of the 2013 Lampedusa disaster, in which hundreds of migrants died in the sinking of a fishing boat off the coast of the Sicilian island. The passengers in the boat were mostly Eritrean, and in this shape-shifting and cinematic work the poet imagines them together on the night ocean, singing hymns to the Virgin Mary to ward off disaster. The poem then focusses on an individual and personal tragedy: the death of Yohanna as she was in the act of giving birth, still joined to her dead child. The ululations that resound within the poem to celebrate the birth become at the same moment the sounds of mourning for the dead mother and baby.

What is odd and astonishing about this poem are its simultaneous multiple perspectives on the tragedy. The voice is by turns a sober documentary narrator recalling the events of the night; then a witness, right there, amongst the people, listening to Yohanna's partner, Mebrahtom, calling her name in desperation; then circling above the boat, lamenting the fate of the Eritrean people and ululating, in the place of those who should have attended Yohanna's birth.

'Lampedusa' is an act of witness – the narrator of the poem seems to have been on the boat with her fellow Eritreans and she has come back to tell us how they died. It's contemporary in its filmic approach, yet it employs the heightened rhetoric of Biblical narrative, the exclamatory style of a public mourner. The poet mourns the deaths of a people, her people, in a rich and stately poem which is also also fervent and full of indignant horror.

In May 2016 Ribka came to the UK to read 'Lampedusa' at the Brighton Festival. She read together with the Eritrean performer Niyat Asfaha, who read the English translation. In live performance the varied sound textures of the poem were very apparent: the two women wove English, Italian and Eritrean into a single multi-lingual lament, with Ribka singing the hymns in the text and ululating passionately. It was a moving and memorable performance of a poem that desires above all to communicate its tragedy, and unsurprisingly many people in the audience were touched to tears.

Earlier in the day Ribka had visited a local Brighton school, where children in year seven had been reading and studying her poem. The children had prepared various performances around the poem: one group giving a group performance from a boat they had 'built' from desks and chairs, and another group reading out monologues they had written from the point of view of Eritrean migrants on the boat. This last exercise, as very occasionally happens, had released a sort of magic: Ribka had talked about the political repression and turmoil in Eritrea and the kids had then gone online to choose Eritrean names and research Eritrean life. The resulting short pieces they wrote were surprisingly full of knowledge and empathy. One child, (who, according to his teachers, hadn't ever shown much interest in school work) wrote particularly imaginatively about the persecution and imprisonment 'his' family had suffered before they had decided to flee, and Ribka was delighted – enfolding the boy in her arms, wreathed in warm smiles, she praised his careful research, the way he seemed to know about Eritrea, as if he'd lived there. I could tell that she had made this boy's day – he was transformed and shone with the glory of his success. It was clear that she had a gift for encouraging and responding to the children and explaining Eritrean history in simple ways they could understand, and they loved her for it.

Ribka's poetry is an integral part of her life's mission. Her passionate empathy, her desire to communicate both indignation and love, seem to me to be at the root of her poetry. It does not diminish her work in any way to say that it goes hand-in-hand with her activism, the work she now does on behalf of migrants in her adopted country, Italy. As an advocate and voice for migrants in local government organisations, she translates the experience of migrants and makes it visible – and in her poetry she uses the fine rhetoric of an ancient oral poetic tradition to convey the same sense of unrighted wrongs and political iniquities.

The selection here shows Ribka's use of various forms and registers. It includes political parables and origin tales. In some cases these are directed at a particular audience, who will understand their shape and feel the force of their political anger. I have read the same style of political and religious 'fables' by the Ethiopian poets Alemu Tebeje and Bewketu Seyoum (in translations by Chris Beckett) and I am tantalised by them, not knowing exactly to whom they refer, nor sharing those political insights which might make me applaud, or nod my recognition. But I feel very strongly their magnetism, it draws me in, I do not precisely need to know who the tyrant is to know that the line between tyrant and subject is drawn finely, with creativity, grace and humour – because tyranny has no power over those human qualities. The poetry that arises in a tyranny will often redress a balance we, who stand outside the situation and see only the abstraction of victimhood, cannot feel.

The lyric and personal pieces in *Aulò! Aulò! Aulò!* are expansive and melancholy. In 'Virginity' the speaker wryly comments on gender inequality through a particularly shocking incident. Although the story is told from the position of safety, and with a retrospective anecdotal and distanced quality, in fact it is only her cunning that saves her from a terrifying forced marriage to a strange man. By demonstrating that her own personal sense of worth lies outside the conventions imposed on her fellow women, their prized virginity of no use to her (she uses the excuse of having been raped to avoid being married), she exposes the hypocrisies of the conventional: the man is forced to return to his own 'violated virgin'.

The character of a wanderer, a risk-taker, an exiled teller-of-tales, so often the male voice, professional rhetorician, is occupied here by a woman:

> It was September and winding
> my way, sad and lonely,
> among houses and churches,
> I smelt the incense
> and heard the new year's songs.

('To the Sycamore')

Women have been historically so sequestered and voiceless that this woman's voice, writing of the pain at being apart from her home and community and fated to wander, surprises and impresses me with its singularity and strength of purpose. Although it holds a lonely lament, it is a voice of strength and resilience and generosity – and it is exhilarating to hear the range and power of the voice, however much I can feel its underlying pain.

Ribka Sibhatu is one of few poets to write across more than one language, in her case Tigrinya, Amharic and her adopted Italian. Because an audience matters to her, being an advocate for her people, and yet living in exile, she translates her poetry herself into Italian. It is hard to talk about tone in translation (despite André's translations appearing to be very eloquently true to their source), but I find the tone and perspectives of 'African Grandmothers', fascinating and elusive. As in 'Lampedusa' we have a multiplicity of perspectives: the close-up individual portrait, the old woman reading and minding her cats, with the short lines of the lyric conveying some of the unadorned simplicity of the scene – and then the pulling back of the camera, to show the heavens, and the genetic equivalent of the ancient and distant stars:

> the names and
> the surnames
> of our African grandmothers
> whom Darwin declined
> to mention in his book.

So much is compressed into these four lines: the losses of history, particularly of the nameless women, ancestors, who disappeared into nameless graves, but also, with the mention of Darwin, the sense of a female African history consciously denied by a male, rational and European science. We might also contrast the living, the oral transmission of old woman to younger woman, with the dead word of the book in which Darwin has 'declined' to include such existences.

I am reminded here of Ribka and Niyat's performance, the two voices in Brighton, and the sense of quickness, of language as a living texture. These are fine poems, built for travel, and transmission, and binding the disparate world into a community.

Sasha Dugdale

Notes on the poems

'Lampedusa' – The overwhelming majority of the ship's five hundred and eighteen passengers were Eritrean. – RS

'Now No One Sings Hosannas: An Open Letter' – The Ethiopian Prime Minister Abiy Ahmed, to whom this poem is addressed, arrived at one of the crucial moments in the history of Ethiopian/Eritrean relations with words of peace, love, justice and unity. Many of us were hopeful and Abiy was acclaimed by an overwhelming majority, reflected in the epithet 'Aboy', a term of endearment meaning 'father' and playing on the prestige afforded to his predecessor Aboy Sebhat. We hoped Abiy would usher in a period of reconciliation and religious and social tolerance. Abiy's own Muslim surname, in such a Christian-dominated land, seemed to speak to the peaceful coexistence of earlier times, when disciples of Muhammad had been protected by the Abyssinians.

But Abiy's actions did not follow his rhetoric. Abiy publicly embraced, legitimized and 'crowned' Mr. Isaias Afewerki, the so-called Eritrean president, referred to in the poem by the common abbreviation 'Isu'. Isaias has been in power since the country's independence in 1991, without ever winning an election. In 1998 he declared war on Ethiopia, forestalling the application of fixed-term presidencies agreed in the 1997 constitution, and causing unspeakable pain to my people. The United Nations' 'Commission of Inquiry on human rights in Eritrea' found 'systematic, widespread and gross violations of human rights' in the country throughout his regime.

Abiy has also failed to support Eritrean refugees in the Tigray region, while stoking tensions at home. His actions toward dissenting voices are not what we should expect of a recipient of the Nobel Peace Prize.

I still hope that Abiy will change course and go down in the history as a leader who managed to avoid the balkanization of the region, staying true to his original words of peace and reconciliation. I am reminded of two sayings common to all Abyssinians, that is, Eritreans and Ethiopians alike:

የተናገሩት ከሚጠፋ የወለዱት ይጥፋ ፤ *It is better to lose your own child than your word.*
እውነትና ንጋት እያደር ይገለጣል ፤ *The truth and the dawn appear with time.*

– RS

'The Exact Number of Stars' – 'Wančia' is a cone-shaped container usually fashioned out of an animal horn that is used as a receptacle for drinks, as well as a measuring unit. 'Ṭaff' is a grain smaller than flax that is gluten-free, rich in fibre and calcium. – ANS

'Virginity' – 'Wonciò' is a type of blanket made of rough wool, black, normally used for the traditional sauna reserved for women. – ANS

'My Abebà' – 'Aghelghel' is a traditional woven basket fashioned out of palm fronds. 'Ĥmbascà' is a type of Eritrean bread baked on special occasions; while preparatory methods vary from region to region, it is usually round, thick and soft and can be both sweet and savoury. It is usually served in an aghelghel. – ANS

'To the Sycamore' – Himbirti is a small hilltop village twenty miles from the capital, Asmara. – ANS

Ribka Sibhatu is a poet, writer and human-rights activist. She was born in 1962 in Asmara. At seventeen she was imprisoned for refusing to marry an Ethiopian miltary officer. Self-exiled from Eritrea since 1982, she has lived in Ethiopia, France and Italy. She works as a court interpreter in Rome. Her much-admired book of poems, *Aulò! Canto poesia dall'Eritrea* (Sinnos), was published in 1993 and revised and expanded in 2009. In 2011 she published a bilingual edition of Tigrinya folklore, *Il numero esatto delle stelle* (Sinnos). Her life, told through the experience of her migration, was the subject of the 2012 documentary *Aulò: Roma postcoloniale*. Her work has been anthologized internationally, including in *The World Record: International voices from Southbank Centre's Poetry Parnassus* (Bloodaxe, 2012) and *The Heart of a Stranger: An Anthology of Exile Literature* (Pushkin Press, 2020).

André Naffis-Sahely is the author of the collection T*he Promised Land: Poems from Itinerant Life* (Penguin, 2017) and the pamphlet *The Other Side of Nowhere* (Rough Trade Books, 2019). He is also the editor of *The Heart of a Stranger: An Anthology of Exile Literature* (Pushkin Press, 2020). He is from Abu Dhabi, but was born in Venice to an Iranian father and an Italian mother. He has translated over twenty titles of fiction, poetry and non-fiction, including works by Honoré de Balzac, Émile Zola, Abdellatif Laâbi, Tahar Ben Jelloun and Frankétienne.

Sasha Dugdale is a poet, translator and playwright. She has published four collections of poetry, most recently *Joy* (Carcanet, 2017). In 2017 she was awarded a Cholmondeley Prize. Between 2012 and 2017 she was editor of *Modern Poetry in Translation*. She is co-director of the Winchester Poetry Festival.

About the Poetry Translation Centre

Set up in 2004, the Poetry Translation Centre is the only UK organisation dedicated to translating, publishing and promoting contemporary poetry from Africa, Asia and Latin America. We introduce extraordinary poets from around the world to new audiences through books, online resources and bilingual events. We champion diversity and representation in the arts, and forge enduring relations with diaspora communities in the UK. We explore the craft of translation through our long-running programme of workshops which are open to all.

The Poetry Translation Centre is based in London and is an Arts Council National Portfolio organisation. To find out more about us, including how you can support our work, please visit: www.poetrytranslation.org.

About the World Poet Series

The *World Poet Series* offers an introduction to some of the world's most exciting contemporary poets in an elegant pocket-sized format. The books are presented as bilingual editions, with the English and original-language text displayed side by side. The translations themselves are specially commissioned and completing each book is an afterword essay by a UK-based poet, responding to the translations.